A GUIDE TO ハワイのポピュラーな木へのガイド
HAWAII'S POPULAR TREES

When Mother Nature turned her attention to the Hawaiian Islands, she created a unique living laboratory of flora and fauna unlike anything on earth. The ancestors of Hawaii's present plants and wildlife were brought here by wind and water or carried as seeds by birds, in many cases from islands and atolls long since submerged. In the absence of competition from other plants and animals, they evolved into species unique to these islands. It has been said that had Charles Darwin visited Hawaii before the Galapagos Islands, he would only have written about Hawaii!

Unfortunately, with a few notable exceptions, Hawaii's plants are not particularly spectacular and so attract little support for their conservation or cultivation. Consequently, Hawaii's gardens, streets, and parks are filled with exotic tree species from all over the world. Although a few trees, such as the kukui, coconut, and possibly the hala, were introduced from the South Pacific by the early migrating Polynesians, most of Hawaii's popular trees were introduced after the islands' discovery by Captain James Cook in 1778. They can be found wherever man has seen fit to change his environment.

This guide is intended as an introduction to the amazing assortment of trees to be found in Hawaii.

1

レインボー・シャワー
RAINBOW SHOWER
Cassia javanica x fistula
Tropical Asia

This hybrid, produced in Hawaii many years ago, is one of the most beloved trees in the islands. Although colors vary from almost white to deep pink, the form known as "rainbow shower" has a profusion of magnificent flowers with petals of pink, orange, and red. The

Golden Shower (*C fistula* L.), Tropical ,
ゴールデン・シャワーの
has orange-yellow flowers followed b huge, pendulous p up to 2 feet long. trees are at their b from spring to fall when they are a c mon sight along th streets of Honolul

ア・レフア
I'A-LEHUA
rosideros collina (Forst.)
ssp. polymorpha
vaii

his colorful and
ndant native tree is
first woody plant to
ablish itself on new
a flows, where it re-
ins a stunted bush.
t with more soil and
isture, it can reach
feet or more in
ght. Its petal-less
wers are composed
a large mass of
ghtly colored sta-
ns. Picking these
wers upon entering
untains is said to
ng rain because it
ets the goddess Pele.
e flowers are also an
portant source of
tar for Hawaii's rare
demic birds.

3

オオギバショウ
TRAVELLER'S TREE
Ravenala madagascariensis Gmel.
Madagascar

With its enormous leaves that form in the shape of a fan on top of its tall trunk, this plant looks like a huge, flattened banana. In fact, it is a relative. Huge, green, boat-like bracts arise from the leaf axils and enclose the whitish flowers. It is said that fresh water can always be found at the base of the leaves, hence its common name, traveller's tree.

Travelers Palm

蘭の木
ORCHID TREE
Bauhinia Purpurea (L.)
India and China

The orchid-like flow-
ers of this 20-foot tree
and its many related
species have given rise
to the name "Poor
man's orchid." This
strong plant will toler-
ate quite poor, dry soil
and is a popular land-
scape tree in Hawaii.
The showy flowers, red-
dish purple to
maroon, are
produced throughout
the spring and
summer months.

KUKUI ククイ
Aleurites moluccana (L.) Willd.
Pacific, Tropical Asia

Because it is so abun-
dant and well-known,
few Hawaii residents
would believe that the
kukui is not a native
tree. It was first import-
ed by the early Poly-
nesians because of its
many uses. Kukui nuts
are rich in oil and were
used as candles or
made into leis. The
roots and shell of the
fruit yield a black dye.
When baked, the ker-
nels are edible, but
when raw make a
potent laxative.

フクベの木
CALABASH TREE
Crescentia cujete L.
Tropical America

The calabash tree has a short trunk and spreading branches bearing narrow leaves and bell-shaped flowers. The strange round fruit, each between 6 and 12 inches in diameter, are green when young, but turn black when ripe. They are thick shelled and contain many seeds embedded in pulp.

Today, the fruit are sometimes hollowed out and used as rattles. When polished, the shells make attractive ornaments.

KOA コア
Acacia koa Gray
Hawaii

The koa tree is high prized in Hawaii for it beautifully grained wood. This has resulte in the cutting of many of the largest trees for furniture, serving bowl and decorative pieces. Very large specimens, sometimes up to 50 fe or more, can still be seen in the mountain areas of the island of Hawaii. The koa tree frequently mentioned Hawaiian legends and songs.

スクランブル・エッグの木；カラモナ

**SCRAMBLED EGG TREE;
KALAMONA**
Cassia surattensis Burm.f.
India to E. Polynesia

This is an attractive and colorful shrub or small tree.

Orange-yellow flowers are borne in continuous profusion at the ends of slender arching branches, reminiscent of scrambled eggs!

The bluish-green leaves are divided into 8-16 pairs of leaflets and flat pods, 2-6" long, persist on the plant.

The bark is said to be useful in curing diabetes.

ナツメヤシ
DATE PALM
Phoenix dactylifera L.
North Africa

This famous palm from North Africa has a great many uses. In addition to its well-known edible fruit, the leaves are used for thatching and woven items, and sugar and wine are made from the sap. As the plants are drought tolerant they are invaluable for landscaping in dry areas in Hawaii.

カエンボク
AFRICAN TULIP
Spathodea campanulata Beauv.
Tropical Africa

From late spring to fall, majestic trees often 70 feet tall can be seen bearing large clusters of erect red flowers on branch tips. This is the stately African tulip, one of the most spectacular of tropical trees. The cone-shaped fruit contain numerous seeds surrounded by papery bracts that are distributed by the wind. Unfortunately, this has enabled the tree to enter some of Hawaii's native forests, where it threatens to become an unwelcome invader.

ペーパー・バーク
PAPER BARK
Melaleuca leucadendron L.
Southeast Asia to Australia

The bark of this small tree, the source of its common name, is quite spectacular. It peels off in papery layers, creating a most attractive effect. This adaptive tree does well when in boggy locations, and also in drier areas. The wood is used for firewood and fenceposts, and medicines are made from the leaves.

MANGO マンゴ
Mangifera indica L.
Malaysia

Few have not heard
of the exotic mango,
one of the notable
fruits of the tropics. There
are dozens of varieties in Hawaii, some introduced and
some locally bred.
Opinions vary greatly as
to which is best. The
mango is a large tree,
reaching 70 feet or
more in height. It is an
excellent shade tree.

GUAVA グアバ
Psidium guajava L.
Tropical America

Introduced shortly after Captain Cook's arrival, the guava quickly gained popularity for its lemon-shaped, yellowish fruit, which are produced year-round. The tree can be easily identified by its multicolored trunk, oblong leaves, and white flowers. The pulp of the fruit is pink or cream and can be eaten raw, but it is more commonly used to make the famous guava juice.

ベンガル・ボダイジュ
INDIAN BANYAN
Ficus benghalensis L.
India

This is the most spectacular of the many banyans in Hawaii because of its massive aerial root system. The roots are produced to support new growth as the tree branches outward. Much of the tree's appeal lies in the maze of passages that the roots of large specimens produce. A banyan at Lahaina, Maui, covers well over half an acre!

JACARANDA ジャカランダ
Jacaranda acutifolia Humb. & Bonpl.
Peru

In late spring and early summer, especially in cooler locations, the jacaranda comes into its own. It bears fern-like leaves and beautiful purple-blue bell-shaped flowers in huge clusters at the ends of branches. These are followed by roundish, wavy, flattened fruit.

PLUMERIA プルメリア
plumeria hybrids

Modern plumerias are hybrids of several tropical American species. They are often called "frangipani" in other parts of the world. The highly scented flowers, produced nearly year round in shades of white, pink, red, and yellow, are prized for leis. The plant possesses an abundance of sticky white juice said to have medicinal properties.

PAPAYA パパイヤ
Carica papaya L.
South America

Better known in many parts of the world as "papaw," this tree is prized for its attractive appearance and delicious fruit. The fruit are yellowish when ripe and are often eaten with lemon juice or in a fresh fruit compote. The small round seeds have a strong peppery taste and are sometimes added to salads in island homes. Unripe fruit can be boiled like potatoes, and the leaves can be crushed on meat as a tenderizer.

COCONUT　ココナッツ
Cocos nucifera L.
South Pacific, Tropical Asia

The coconut is one of the most useful plants in the world, producing shade, construction materials, food, oil, bowls, and fiber. It was introduced to Hawaii by the early Polynesians, who had several varieties. Coconut palms can reach a height of 100 feet and, although often growing on sandy beaches with little or no soil, can withstand hurricanes with ease. The mature nuts are enclosed in a fibrous husk, and when ripe they come crashing to the ground. Because of this, mature nuts are rarely seen on trees in public places in Hawaii — they are removed while still young.

NK TECOMA ピンク・テコマ
Tabebuia pentaphylla (L.) Hemsl.
Tropical America

Pink tecoma is a
popular island tree. It is
distinguished by its pro-
fusion of pink flowers,
borne in small clusters
at branch tips and
produced at intervals
throughout the year.
The trees are especially
beautiful when grown
as single specimens on
lawns, the fallen petals
creating a pink carpet
beneath the tree.

21

COFFEE コーヒー
Coffea arabica L.
Tropical Africa

This shrub or small tree with glossy oval leaves bears pure white, strongly scented flowers. A plant in full bloom in late spring is a spectacular sight. After flowering, small, oval red berries or "beans" are produced. They must be harvested by hand as they mature unevenly. *Coffee arabica* is the source of the famous **Kona** coffee from the island of Hawaii. Both flavorful and expensive, it is enjoyed by connoisseurs the world over.

マカデミア・ナッツ

MACADAMIA NUT
Macadamia integrifolia Maiden and Betche
Australia

Although widely grown in other parts of the world, the macadamia has become synonymous with Hawaii. The first trees were planted in 1890, but only in the last twenty years have the nuts become an important part of Hawaii's economy. The round, hard-shelled nuts are about 1 inch in diameter. They are harvested from the ground after falling naturally.

AVOCADO アボカド
Persea americana Mill.
Tropical America

The avocado, prized for its strong-tasting fruit, was an early introduction to Hawaii. By careful selection among the many varieties, one can have fruiting trees almost all year round. The trees yield a useful oil and some parts have medicinal properties.

ホウオウボク
ROYAL PONCIANA
Delonix regia (Bojer) Ra
Madagascar

Facing extinction its native land, this cies was "saved" b horticulturists, who planted it in tropic countries worldwid The spreading tree all or most of its f like leaves in early spring, to be follo by a blaze of red ers and new green leaves. Appropriate is called "flamboy in many parts of t tropics.

BANANA バナナ
Musa x paradisiaca L.
Old World Tropics

When Captain Cook arrived in Hawaii he found at least fifty varieties of banana already growing there, some of them unique. But until the "kapu" was broken in 1819, women were permitted to eat only two kinds of banana. Like the coconut, the banana plant has many uses. The trunk is a mass of fibers from which rope can be made. The huge leaves make handy umbrellas, plates, or thatch, and have many other uses. After fruiting the trunk dies, but new shoots arise from the base.

MAHOGANY　マホガニー

Swietenia mahogani (L.) Jacq.
S. Florida & W. Indies

A handsome tree often more than 60 ft. high with large buttress roots at the base. It is a popular street and landscape plant in many tropical areas.

The shiny leaves are made up of 4-8 pairs of leaflets, each 1-3″ long. Flowers, small and white, are borne in profusion at the ends of wide-spreading branches. The flat winged seeds, from which this tree is most easily grow, are contained in a 2-4″ long woody capsule.

Mahogany wood is prized for many uses including the manufacture of furniture and musical instruments.

アメリカネムの木
MONKEYPOD
Samanea saman (Jacq.) Merr.
Tropical America

Monkeypod wood is known to most poeple from the beautiful carved bowls and ornaments found everywhere in Hawaii. Less familiar is the tree, with its huge umbrella shape and massive trunk. Its feather-like leaves close up in the evening and in rainy weather, giving it an alternative common name, "rain tree." Another unusual trait is that most trees lose most or all their leaves early in the spring.

アンブレラ・ツリー
UMBRELLA TREE
Brassaia actinophylla Endl.
Australia

This odd-looking tree has large umbrella-shaped leaves made up of several long leaflets at the ends of branches. When in flower, long, widely spreading floral branches bearing unique small clusters of red flowers have given it the name "octopus tree." The seeds germinate readily and can often be found growing in the forks of large trees or on the ground. For this reason they are unpopular with gardeners, who have to contend with the rapidly growing plants.

HALA ハラ
Pandanus odoratissimus L.f.
Pacific to East Asia

This strange branching tree can be seen along the shores of all islands. Its long narrow, spine-edged leaves, aerial roots, and large fruits resembling pineapples all combine to make this a most unique and primitive tree. The leaves, "lauhala," are used in making mats, sandals, hats, and baskets throughout the Pacific. They can also be used for thatching.

29

パンの木
BREADFRUIT
Artocarpus altilis L.
Malaysia

Dozens of varieties of breadfruit are found throughout the Pacific, and the early Polynesians brought one form to Hawaii. The warty-skinned fruit ca up to 10 pound are more or le and about 10 i long. The tough skin covers a s flesh that is qu cious when bak steamed.

ソーセージの木
SAUSAGE TREE
Kigelia africana Benth.
Tropical West Africa

The sausage tree is an oddity in Hawaiian gardens. Its strange flowers are reminiscent of raw meat. They are followed by long, broad sausage-shaped fruit, which are inedible although said to be of medicinal use in Africa.

金の木
GOLD TREE
Tabebuia donnell-smithii Rose
Central America

From early in the year to July or August, tall leafless trees covered with masses of yellow flowers can be seen along streets and highways. This is the famous "gold tree." Only after flowering are the pale-green leaves produced.

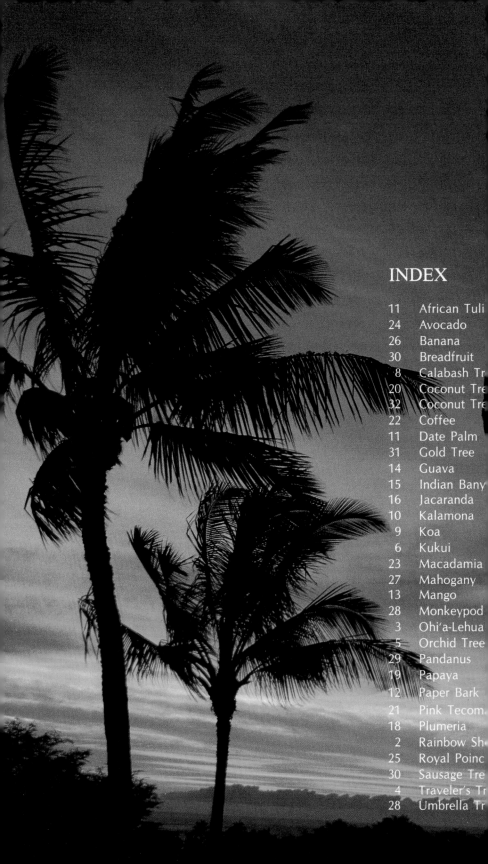

INDEX